A Sweet Lemon

Arrives at Two Mountain Farm

Karen E. Rose

Copyright © 2015 Karen E. Rose
All rights reserved.
No part of this book may be reproduced
without the consent of the author.
ISBN-13: 978-1517071745
ISBN-10: 1517071747

To All The Underdogs.

We cheer them on.
We love to root for them.
And there's nothing better than
a great underdog story.

Here is Lemon's.

When we last left them . . . .

Pixie and Fenway
Had drifted off to sleep,
Wondering what new friends
On the farm they might meet.
Could they ever imagine,
Or dream it to be?
A tiny little chicken
With no eyes to see.
How would she make it?
What would she do?
Pixie and Fenway,
They wondered this too.
So in your cozy seat
With a listening ear,
A true underdog tale,
Is what you will hear.

The Farm Mom was so excited!

Today was the day that the new baby chicks arrived at Two Mountain Farm.

As she watched the new little fluff balls run around in their coop, she noticed one that was much smaller than the rest.

When the Farm Mom picked this little one up, she noticed something very different; this little chick had no eyes.

NO EYES!!!

What was the Farm Mom to do?
She decided to bring this little chick into the farm house and place her in her own small coop. The Farm Mom watched this little, fluffy, yellow chick in her new coop and said, "I will call her Lemon."

As the Farm Mom was making sure that Lemon was settled in, Fenway came down to see what was going on. He had heard that there were new chicks arriving at the farm but now, there was one in the house and his Farm Mom looked worried.

Fenway went onto the screened porch and called to Pixie in her coop, "Pixie, come quick!"

"What's wrong Fenway?"

"The new chicks arrived today and there is one in the farm house with no eyes," said Fenway.

"What?" Pixie clucked loudly, "No eyes?"

"Yes, she is little, fluffy, yellow, her name is Lemon, and she has no eyes," Fenway meowed back.

"I am worried," said Pixie, "If she has no eyes and cannot see, how will she find her food?"

"And how will she be able to find her water to drink?" questioned Fenway, "What should we do Pixie?"

"Since Lemon is inside the farm house, why don't you look out for her and keep me posted," replied Pixie.

"I will do that," said Fenway as he trotted back inside the farm house.

Each day, Fenway watched as the Farm Mom worked with Lemon; teaching her how to eat, showing her where her water was, and helping her adjust to her little coop.

Every evening, Fenway would report Lemon's progress to Pixie. "Pixie, Lemon is finally eating on her own!" Fenway said with excitement, "She has even discovered her water and can drink. Our Farm Mom keeps everything the same for her; her water is always on the left and her food on the right so she can find it easily."

"That is wonderful news Fenway," said Pixie, "It sounds like Lemon is not letting the fact that she has no eyes and cannot see keep her from being just like any other little chick. Go Lemon, Go!" clucked Pixie.

As the weeks passed, the Farm Mom was pleased with how Lemon was adjusting and settling in. Lemon's baby chick fuzz started to disappear and her feathers started to grow. She was eating, drinking and getting bigger each day.

Even though Lemon was growing and doing well, Fenway always stayed close to keep watch over her. He would often lie next to her little coop inside the farm house to keep her company. "Lemon, I know you cannot see me but my name is Fenway, I am a cat, and I am going to be your friend. I have another chicken friend named Pixie and I sure hope you get to meet her soon."

"Hi Fenway," cheeped little Lemon, "Thank you for keeping me company; it's so nice to know that I have a friend."

As Fenway wished, the Farm Mom soon brought Lemon out onto the screened porch for some fresh air.

Pixie was so excited that she walked right over to Lemon and said, "Well hello little one, my name is Pixie and I am a chicken just like you."

"Hi Pixie," chirped Lemon, "Fenway has told me about you and it is nice to meet you."

Now that Pixie was able to see Lemon up close, she was able to see Lemon's sweet face with no eyes. Pixie also noticed that Lemon was as happy as could be. She cheeped and wandered around the screened porch without a care as she explored.

Pixie asked Lemon, "How are you doing in your coop inside the farm house?"

"I am doing just fine," Lemon replied. "It was difficult at first but our Farm Mom helped me and made sure that I ate and drank and now I can do it all by myself," Lemon said proudly. I discovered where everything is in my coop by feeling my way around with my beak."

"That is wonderful Lemon," clucked Pixie.

The Farm Mom then came to collect Lemon and bring her back into the farm house.

"See you soon," Pixie called after Lemon.

Months passed and Lemon grew, boy did she grow!

She grew tail feathers, wing feathers, and her baby chick cheeping was turning into clucking. Lemon was growing too big for her coop inside the farm house so the Farm Mom asked the Farm Dad to build Lemon a permanent coop on the screened porch with Pixie where she would have plenty of room.

The Farm Dad built Lemon a beauty of a coop. It was nice and big and had lots of things that were built in and stable so that they could not get knocked over. Just like in her little coop, Lemon's water was on the left and her food was on the right. She also had a nice roost where she could sleep.

When Lemon moved out to the screened porch in her new coop, Pixie got a new coop as well. The Farm Dad built Pixie a coop just like Lemon's; Pixie now had the bottom coop with a new neighbor and friend in Lemon who was in the top coop.

As the weeks passed, Lemon settled in to her new coop on the screened porch. Pixie and Fenway soon discovered that Lemon did everything that any other chicken would do. She scratched at the ground, she preened her feathers to keep them clean and soft, she went to her roost to sleep at night, and she took dust baths.

Each morning, the Farm Mom would let Lemon out of her coop to spend some time with Pixie and Fenway on the screened porch.

On many mornings, Pixie would get a special treat at breakfast that she enjoyed while Fenway would drink from Pixie's water bowl. One morning, the Farm Mom gave Pixie a bowl of apple slices for a treat. When the Farm Mom returned from letting the other chickens out of the coop, she found Pixie and Lemon sharing the bowl of apples. Lemon had heard Pixie eating from the bowl and it made a "plink" sound as she ate. So, Lemon followed the sound and discovered a delicious snack that Pixie was more than happy to share with her.

Lemon found her way around the screened porch by listening and feeling her way with her beak. One day while Fenway was looking out the window at the chipmunks and squirrels, Lemon snuck up behind Fenway. When Fenway turned around, he was nose to beak with Lemon.

"Hey, hey, hey Lemon," Fenway said, "that's a little too close for me. I need a little more personal space."

"Sorry Fenway," Lemon replied, "I felt your fur but didn't know how close I was."

Pixie chuckled, "You were too busy watching outside and a little chicken snuck up and scared a big cat like you! " Lemon giggled as she backed away and continued exploring.

When the weather was nice and the Farm Mom was outside, Lemon and Pixie were allowed out in the yard. They would nibble on the grass, peck at the ground to find bugs, and enjoy the warmth of the sun.

"You sure are good at catching bugs," Pixie said to Lemon.

"I cannot see them, but I know that if I work hard enough, keep trying, and continue pecking at the ground, I will find them," Lemon clucked as she gobbled up a juicy bug.

The seasons soon changed and one cooler morning when Fenway came downstairs, he heard lots of noise coming from the screened porch. From inside Lemon's coop he heard, "BAWK, BAWK, SQUAK, SQUAK!"

Fenway called to Pixie, "Why is Lemon being so noisy this morning?"

"She is just singing her egg song," replied Pixie.

Fenway had never heard of such a thing.
"What's an egg song?" he asked.

"Well, some hens will sing a song to announce that they are going to lay an egg. So, I would say that Lemon is going to lay her first egg," said Pixie.

And sure enough, later that day, the Farm Mom went out to the screened porch to discover Lemon sitting proudly next to her first egg.

The Farm Mom held Lemon's warm egg in her hand and smiled knowing that Lemon did everything that any other chicken in the flock did, and she did it with no eyes.

Pixie and Fenway stood next to their Farm Mom proud of their friend Lemon as well.

Pixie turned toward Fenway and said, "Look at us Fenway, no one thought we would be friends because we are different. Lemon is different too because she has no eyes. But all Lemon needed was some help adjusting from our Farm Mom, a nice living space from our Farm Dad, kindness from two new friends like us, and a chance to be a chicken. All she needed was a chance."

Fenway smiled and meowed back, "I sure am glad that Lemon got that chance."

"I am too," clucked Lemon from her roost in her coop, "and I could not ask for two nicer friends. I am a lucky chicken."

"And we are lucky to have you as a friend too," said Fenway as Pixie clucked in agreement.

Pixie then went into her coop and settled in for the night. Lemon was already perched on her roost and ready for bed, and Fenway trotted back into the farm house behind the Farm Mom ready for a long cat nap after the day's excitement.

Pixie, Fenway, and Lemon all needed a good night's sleep because tomorrow was sure to be another fun filled day at Two Mountain Farm.

With Much Gratitude To:

Bryan – you allowed Lemon to live in the house for three months and have come to embrace the notion that the screened porch has evolved into an auxiliary chicken coop, avian ambulatory care and recovery center, and poultry maternity ward. I am so grateful that I have a partner who accepts me and all of my eccentricities and regiments when it comes to the care of our animals – much love

Pixie and Fenway – the real characters who started it all. They are two kind hearted animal souls who accept each other and taught us a sweet and fundamental lesson in the process. I am so lucky to be able to watch that friendship each day.

Lemon – who taught me a bit more patience and shows me every day that love is truly blind.

All the fans of Pixie, Fenway, and Lemon who were so supportive of my first book and encouraged me to write a second one.

Missy Feeney from Millard Hawk Primary School in Central Square, New York, and Allyson Hoffman from Molly Stark Elementary School in Bennington, Vermont who were so kind to allow me to read *Pixie & Fenway* to their classes and enthusiastically encouraged their students to draw for this book.

The numerous kid artists who took a story about a chicken with no eyes and gave it a unique and creative visual voice.

Mom and Dad – you are two people who continue to "show up" for me. From swimming lessons, to ballet recitals, violin performances, plays, soccer games, synchronized swimming shows, and college lacrosse games, you always showed up. And, I am still so lucky that you continue to show up for me; attending readings and events, filling in with kitty sitting and chicken chores, and just supporting me. I am so very fortunate.

☮ My brother Doug – I am a better person for the twenty years I had with you. The girl who used to go hiking with you in full makeup is now the girl who wears none, lives on a farm, and hugs chickens. I think you would be highly amused and genuinely proud. I hope you are smiling at all of this and I truly thank you for being my friend.

With Special Thanks:

I would like to recognize the kids who took a chance on me and a sweet story about unlikely friendship with my first book and who have continued with me on this special journey.

Here's a little more about the artists who participated in illustrating both *Pixie and Fenway – Unlikely Friends at Two Mountain Farm* and *A Sweet Lemon Arrives at Two Mountain Farm*.

Racheal Tripp – Racheal is six years old and lives in Central Square, New York. She is in first grade at Millard Hawk Primary School and her favorite colors are yellow, pink, and light blue. Racheal enjoys coloring, arts and crafts, swimming, ballet, and jumping on trampolines. Her favorite foods are pizza and chocolate chip ice cream. She also has three cats named Popcorn, Shadow, and Cuddles. Racheal held a baby chick for the first time during a visit to Two Mountain Farm in 2012 and someday hopes to have chickens of her own.

Kyra Elizabeth Stratton – Hailing from Bennington, Vermont, Kyra is eight years old and is in third grade at Molly Stark Elementary School. Her hobbies include cheerleading, baton, gymnastics, drawing and writing. Kyra's favorite colors are pink and baby blue and foods that top her list are macaroni & cheese, cheesy hot dogs, and chicken alfredo. Kyra loves animals and has two hamsters named Whitey and Brownie, as well as three dogs; Miley, Merle, and Tank. Kyra enjoys chickens and has assisted her grandmother, Patti, in feeding and tending to the flock at Two Mountain Farm when the Farm Mom and Farm Dad are on vacation.

Haley Lassen – Haley illustrated the covers of both *Pixie & Fenway – Unlikely Friends at Two Mountain Farm* along with this book. Read more about Haley on the back cover.

Index of Artists

In order of illustration appearance

Carter, age 5, Central Square, NY * – page 3
Haley, age 13, Rutland, VT – page 4
Kari, age 8, Walpole, MA – pages 6, 26, 33
Leila, age 8, South Hero, VT – pages 8, 37
Amara, age 10, Bennington, VT ** – page 9
Madysen, age 7, Bennington, VT ** – page 11
Lola, age 7, West Monroe, NY *– page 12
Jasmine, age 11, Bennington, VT ** – page 15
Will, age 9, Manchester, CT – page 16
Caleb, age 7, Clifton Park, NY – page 17
Abigail, age 10, Clifton Park, NY – pages 18, 28
Alexis, age 8, Bennington, VT ** – page 19
Kyra, age 8, Bennington, VT ** – pages 20, 35, 41
Cash, age 8, Bennington, VT ** – page 21
Kevin, age 10, Bennington, VT ** – page 23
Madeline, age 10, Glenmoore, PA – pages 24, 30
Ava C., age 8, Westville, Nova Scotia, Canada – pages 27, 34
Mackenzie, age 4, Vernon, CT – page 28
Racheal, age 6, Central Square, NY * – pages 29, 31, 40
Ava H., age 7, Bennington, VT ** – page 35
Ryan, age 11, Bennington, VT ** – page 36
Julia, age 10, Bennington, VT ** – page 37

* Millard Hawk Primary School Students – Central Square, New York
** Molly Stark Elementary School Students – Bennington, Vermont

Made in the USA
Middletown, DE
15 October 2015